Lucky Lucky the Love Puppy
a read-along, sing-along, feelings picture book

Robin Waters Casper, LMFT (retired)

Hear the Lucky Lucky the Love Puppy Song in English
free on the YouTube Channel: Waters N Light Books

https://youtu.be/z0YnOrWoeMI

Look for the Hawaiian-style Edition:

Lucky Lucky Aloha Puppy.

Song heard free on YouTube:

https://youtu.be/CIzm6HvwNAI

Coming soon in 2018: English/Spanish Edition:

Suerte Suerte el Perrito de Amor

Lucky Lucky the Love Puppy
a read-along, sing-along, feelings picture book

Robin Waters Casper, LMFT
(retired)

Published 2016, First Edition

ISBN: 978-0-692-59085-0 (paperback)
ISBN: 978-0-9974173-1-9 (ebook)

Library of Congress Control Number: 2016904534

The author may be contacted at Waters N Light Books:

Contact Form: www.watersnlight.com

Email: watersnlight@gmail.com

Published in the U.S.A.
Waters N Light Books

For Devin Casper and Alexi Casper

ACKNOWLEDGEMENTS

Thank you to the angels that allowed Lucky to live out his life's purpose as the Love Puppy. I am grateful for the support of my husband, David Casper, LMFT, retired, without whom this book and song never would have manifested, and to Devin and Alexi, our grandchildren, for their participation. The following people played pivotal roles in its development: Heidi Nalley, who writes as Thatcher C. Nalley and Heidi A. Thatcher, sparked the belief that I could indeed self-publish; Tracie Devlin taught me to listen to inner guidance; Gina Trenalone transcribed the melody that sprang forth into musical notation, performed piano, and arranged the connection with Scott Cory, owner of Heirloom Studios in Chico, California; Scott expertly recorded and mixed *Lucky Lucky the Love Puppy Song Audiobook* and the recording produced in digital form now heard free on YouTube. Others also offered valued support: Karla Follestad provided last-minute editing, while Julia Lynn Rose and Jennifer Rhoades were both instrumental in helping me capture Lucky's emotive behaviors. Thanks to the late Dr. John Whitaker, as when I worked in my first clinical job as an MFT Intern, he was my inspiring Clinical Supervisor at Children's Bureau of Southern California where I learned the power of story in therapeutic play. I honor the guidance, feedback, and endorsement from Dr. Joyce C. Mills, Executive Director of StoryPlay Global for my early reader chapter book, *Mindful Max and the Mental Magic Club*, which encouraged me further along the author path. I owe a debt of gratitude to Carole O'Gara, my Clinical Supervisor at Butte County Department of Behavioral Health, Youth Services, for specialized training and for allowing me the honor of providing therapy to very young clients and their caregivers. Carole showed me how interacting with eye contact, healthy touch, stories, games, songs, and playfulness positively impacts wellness, parent/child attunement, and development. The California First Five Commission's commitment to early childhood mental health played a big part in our county's programs, which fueled my interest in providing services. I am filled with gratitude for such an abundant life. I consider myself lucky, not only to have a cute, sweet, and funny dog, but also to bask in the warmth of supportive family and friends. I appreciate all my angels, everywhere, for this project that arose from the highest power of all, Love.

Guide for Parents, Teachers, and Therapists

Hello, my name is Robin Waters Casper, aka Robin L. Waters and Robin L. Casper. I am a California Licensed Marriage and Family Therapist, #41820. This guide is for the emotional education component of *Lucky Lucky the Love Puppy*, a fun, read-along, sing-along, feelings picture book about Lucky, a cute, sweet, and very emotive dog. For five years as a therapist working in Youth Services at our county mental health system, Butte County Department of Behavioral Health, I worked in association with the State of California's First Five Commission, implementing programs designed for children ages 0 to 5. The purpose of my work was to build bonds between parents and children who were often in the court system with the goal of reunification. As a result, children benefited from increased socio-emotional and brain development. This process included interaction with stories, songs, and games in which I made use of concepts from the Theraplay Institute and from Conscious Discipline. At times, the play therapist in me would step up with my own versions of materials.

Lucky Lucky the Love Puppy is a project I created after my time at Behavioral Health had ended. A simple feelings picture book for ages 0 to 6 with a separate companion audio songbook, it offers children and adults an expressive bridge to sharing and discussing emotions. There are several ways to use this program. Children and adults can read the book, sing the song, listen while reading, or sing the song with accompanying gestures. Afterwards, I ask questions that a parent, caregiver, teacher, or therapist can implement for emotional education. The questions are designed to help children identify their feelings, where they feel them in their bodies, what they can do to feel an emotion again or to feel better from a distressful feeling, and how they can use words for both emotional expression and to get along better with others. These are open ended questions that I do not answer. I leave this to parents, caregivers, and teachers to impart their own wisdom and to the many therapists who will find this tool useful for child and parent-child therapy sessions.

However, as a bonus within the context of this guide, I do offer one game of my own creation that I often played with verbal children and/or children and parents, the "I Feel Catch Game" to teach "I statements" in an engaging way. It can be played sitting on the floor or standing across from each other. A soft, regular-sized, children's ball is thrown back and forth, or rolled for younger children. The child throws the ball to the adult who catches it and models the following: "I feel <u>(an emotion)</u> when <u>(a situation that engenders that feeling).</u>" Example: "I feel happy when I spend time playing with you." The adult should ensure the feelings and situations they model are age-appropriate in level of intensity, and, ideally, encourage closeness or are relevant to the family or classroom. The adult then throws the ball to the child and coaches with: "Your turn. Say, 'I feel'," after which the adult waits for the child to repeat, then states "Okay, name a feeling," and waits for an answer. Next the adult states: "…when… now say something that helps you feel that way." Children usually get the hang of it quickly, but if they don't, the adult can pick the feeling and stop after the word, "when", leaving the situation open for the child to fill in with their own. This game can be played at the end of reading or singing *Lucky, Lucky the Love Puppy,* when answering the ensuing questions, or as an unrelated activity.

Lucky and I invite you on an adventure to an awe-inspiring place of emotional growth and connection, a realm of understanding where children learn to express feelings and adults join in while truly listening. Together they discover the compassionate inner world of wonders.

I welcome you to share my vision of all children reaping the rewards of human attachment and developmental wholeness.

Robin Waters Casper, M.A., LMFT
April 2016

Oh, Lucky Lucky, the Love Puppy,

let's tell kids your history.

Oh, Lucky Lucky, the Love Puppy,

you're a pound dog and sweetie.

2

Oh, Lucky Lucky, the Love Puppy,

has brown eyes so round and big.

Oh, Lucky Lucky, the Love Puppy,

and jowls that go crooked.

Oh, Lucky Lucky, the Love Puppy,

has ears that are long and fluffy.

Oh, Lucky Lucky, the Love Puppy,

and gold fur that is shiny.

Oh, Lucky Lucky, the Love Puppy,

how do you act out a feeling?

7

Oh, Lucky Lucky, the Love Puppy,

snuggle close when you're loving.

Oh, Lucky Lucky, the Love Puppy,

poke a paw to get petting.

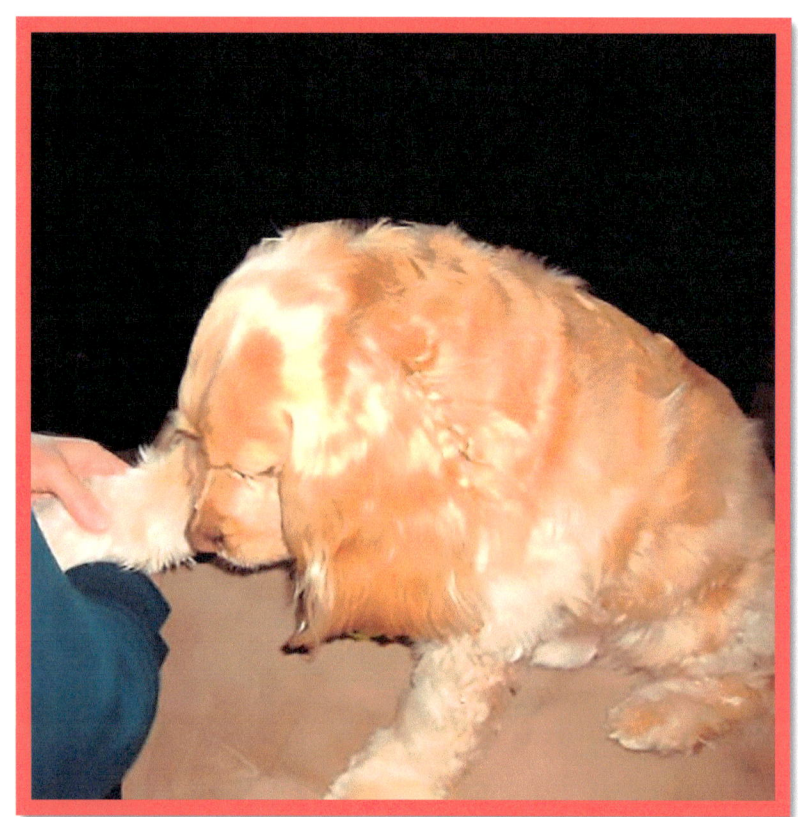

Oh, Lucky Lucky, the Love Puppy,

flop your ears so free running.

10

Oh, Lucky Lucky, the Love Puppy,

pant your tongue when you're happy.

Oh, Lucky Lucky, the Love Puppy,

howl out when you feel sadly.

Oh, Lucky Lucky, the Love Puppy,

chase your ball so playfully.

Oh, Lucky Lucky, the Love Puppy,

droop your eyes when you're lonely.

Oh, Lucky Lucky, the Love Puppy,

slide on floors when you're silly.

15

Oh, Lucky Lucky, the Love Puppy,

hang your head when you're guilty.

Oh, Lucky Lucky, the Love Puppy,

roll on smells when you're funny.

17

Oh, Lucky Lucky, the Love Puppy,

growl so loud when you're angry.

Oh, Lucky Lucky, the Love Puppy,

Dogs don't have the words to use.

Oh, Lucky Lucky, the Love Puppy,

when kids use words, they can't lose.

Oh, Lucky Lucky, the Love Puppy,

kids can act out feelings too.

Oh, Lucky Lucky, the Love Puppy,

let's see what it is they do.

22

Oh, Lucky Lucky, the Love Puppy,

thank you for the joy you bring.

Oh, Lucky Lucky, the Love Puppy,

now it's goodbye that we sing.

Oh, Lucky Lucky, the Love Puppy,

wave so long to everyone.

Oh, Lucky Lucky, the Love Puppy,

see you in our dreams for fun.

The End

Discussion Questions

♥ Hi kids! Now that you know how Lucky acts out his feelings, how do you act when you feel happy, or sad, or mad, or scared, or feelings like surprised, shy, or other ways?

♥ How does your face look when you feel that way?

♥ What kinds of things happen that bring on that feeling?

♥ Where do you feel that in your body? In your head? Eyes? Ears? Nose? Throat? Heart? Tummy? Arms? Legs? Hands? Feet?

♥ What can you do if you want to feel better?

♥ What about if you want to feel this way again?

♥ How can you use your words to help show feelings?

♥ What about to get along better with others?

There are so many feelings and so much to learn about them.
They are like crayons that color our lives:
like rays of a rainbow, all different, but all important.
Thanks for sharing your feelings with Lucky!
Bye for now!

Made in the USA
Monee, IL
07 July 2026